Shattered Illusions

An Anthology of Poetry

Edited by Amanda Read

δ

Published by Dogma Publications

Dogma Publications, Bicester Innovation Centre, Telford Road,
Bicester, Oxon, OX26 4LD

Shattered Illusions

Cover picture taken from Karl Blechen's
Gorge at Amalfi
1831
Nationalgalerie, Berlin

First Published 2006
by Dogma Publications

ISBN: 1-84591-018-4
ISBN 13: 978-1-85491-018-1

Printed in Great Britain for Dogma Publications

Shattered Illusions

Contents

The Story Of Us	Louise Sproat	1
Once	Natasha Liu-Thwaites	2
An April Wedding	B June V Squires	3
All The Paintings Of Us (Have Faded)	Leon Patrick Slater	4
Where Do I Find Love,		
Or Does Love Find Me?	Joanne Alison George	5
Visions Of The Soul	Peter Morris-Webb	6
Growing Old	Christine Smith	8
24/7	Anne M Carter	9
Frustration	Beryl Stone	10
Cat Burglar	Ruth Laughton	12
The Dance	Catherine A Gabbott	13
Believe	Nikki Anne Schmutz	14
She Is Lost	Anna Isaac	15
Birthday	Curtis Tappenden	16
Waiting	Henry Warwick Parkin	17
He Sleeps	Tom Pheby	18
Don't Go Into The Barn	Joe Gardner	19
Gilgamesh	Peter Lewis Holmes	20
Do We But Dimly Perceive?	Stephen Michael McGowan	21
The Heart	Amy Culpepper	22
Eyes Of Suicide	Elizabeth Price	23
Despair	Joseph Parks	24
Tiger Stripes	Lucy Ann Sparrow	25
Generation Gap	Philip J Legood	26
Fit To Drop	Joan L Defraine	28
The Outsider	Lindsay Michael Hayman	29
The Last Big Sigh	David Boyce	30
Addiction	Ellen Jones	31
Letters In Faded Ink	Lee Richard Kirsten	32
The Mist Of Peace	Alison Sutton	33
Love	Jemma Walker	34
Shadow	Joseph David Perry	35
Oh Spring	Katherine Birchall	36
Trafalgar	Bethany McIntosh	37
The Lighthouse	Terry Pratley	38
In Lament Of Sundays	Dolly Chambers	39
Games Special	Edith Blagrove	40
Some Dorset Delights	Sammy "Michael" Davis	41
The Sea	Rowena Haley	42

Contents continued

The Cottage	Jennifer Miller	43
Grandchildren	Barbara Jackson	44
Lessons Of Earth	June Annie Davis	45
You Stole My Heart	Dawn Morris	46
Torment	Calvin White	47
An Enchanting Winters' Day	Phillis Green	48
The Lonely Hours	Jim Lawes	49
Prisoner	Steve Mann	50
A Treasured Memory	Tony Reese	51
The Morning	Michelle Beech	52
The Brightest Star	Christopher Smith	53
My Best Friend	Sheila Smith	54
Options	Tony Wright	55
My Love	Brenda Haines	56
Frozen In Time	Susan Brown	57
Mother Nature	Julia Boyle	58
Will Anything Be Enough?	Sophie Petrie	59
You Don't Care	Maria Jones	60
Fantasia	Jennifer Elisabeth Mace	61
Angel	Mel Moore	62
To My Rival	Eleanor Dawn Howlett	63
Ballymore Holly's Gem	Chris Judge	64
The One	Labi Hassan	66
Unlikely Eden	Amy Barnes	67
Hidden	Olivia Atkinson	68
I'm Lost	Kathleen Bartholomew	69
The Rose	Robert Martin Ricketts	70
Why Oh Why	Michael John McCarron	71
Components	Dolly Parker	72
Chance To Live	Rachael Carrick	73
A Winters' Day	Glenn John Walker	74
Dimensions Of Mind	Anna Kompaniets	75
The Miracle Man	Mahesh Patel	76
Hurt	Claire Ann Wall	78
Lost Soul	Lucy Beams	79
Where Is My Love?	Trissie Burgess	80
One Lost Soul	Caroline Heywood	81
The Green Blanket Beneath My Feet	Clare Lynda Hayman	82
Aching	Lucy Quarrier	83

The Story Of Us

It was in June we met the date escapes me now.
But it was real, you where real
How strange it feels to be sitting here writing this
From the minute I met you I loved you
With a love so fierce it scared me it still does
You never go away, you never leave me be, you are with me always
Not In person but you are imprinted on my heart
I remember the first second I saw you it makes me want to cry
I wonder now if I had know what I do now would I
Have walked away that day turned my back on the boy in blue.
We both know I would not when it comes to you I have no control.
The love I felt then is still in me now
I hide it no one knows it still burns in me.
When your name comes up as it often does
I shrug it of like I feel nothing
If the truth were told the mere mention of your name turns me to jelly.
You loved me too once not so long ago.
You don't now
It was warm that day we met bright and sunny
My days and night are now filled with a coldness I can't escape from
I think the problems lies within my heart
They think I don't love you anymore
They are wrong
My heart aches with a constant pain
My head is filled with you
You are in everything I do
You are in everything that I see
I think the problem is that you are my everything.

Louise Sproat

Once

During moments of dark despair,
Wild-eyed and unhappy,
Thoughts too much to bear,
I found a star in the dark night sky;
I found a jewel that I'd love till I died.

And yet I could not show my love;
Felt locked in a cage like a pretty white dove,
Longing for freedom but feeling trapped.
Angry and bitter, world close to collapse.

I was just about to open the door,
Just about to let my heart soar.
Then I lost the star to the depths of the night,
To the ink of the sky it slipped out of sight.

The jewel was gone; taken from me,
By fate and sadness and melancholy.
I was lost again to the black of the world.
I was lost again, with nowhere to turn.

Yet I was happy, because I had seen that star,
I had loved that jewel, albeit from afar.
Yes, I had loved for once in my life.
And once is enough.
Once still brings light.

Natasha Liu-Thwaites

An April Wedding

An April Wedding like no other,
scorned by some, as mistress, lover,
becomes a princess, consort royal.
Patient lady, strong and loyal.

Entwined initials, heartache, guilt.
The fairytale over, naïve tears spilt.
A tragic loss, a nation weeps
over carpets of flowers, and vigil keeps
with candles burning, lest we forget.
For two young sons, despair, regret.

A royal family torn apart,
from ancient monarchs, the core, the heart
of a rich and pleasant land. A history
engrained in stone, in mountain mists, in mystery.

A Queen as steadfast as the English oak,
a lifetime of duty in crown and cloak.
No torture now, no dungeons find,
but cruelty of a different kind.
Life in a bowl, no stone unturned,
mistakes are made and lessons learned.
A media circus with every event,
unkind words that breed dissent.

A Prince who cares and wins the Trust
to fund young dreams. A farmer, who just
loves the land, no poisons here,
just good rich soil. Yet still they jeer
as snow-covered slopes pick up the sounds
of hurt. More copy for the tabloid hounds.
So while the world will mourn a Pope,
a prince, a wedding, a time of hope.
No faint heart now, but another chance
to heal, to seal, a royal romance.

B June V Squires

3

All The Paintings Of Us (Have Faded)

Sitting in our house I know,
You're not coming back this time.
Ignorance and a broken heart
Can never bring me pride.

The kisses placed on my neck,
They faded so long ago.
I'm reminded of our past lives
By the pictures in our home.

The colour of our sunrise,
It was painted on these walls.
The sheets we slept in blew away
And our curtains all shall fall.

The paintings you gave to me,
Since then they all have faded.
Broken glass from the wines we sipped
With lochs of hair we braided.

The roses in our garden,
Memories of my valentine.
Carpet burns from all of the floors
And all the gifts we declined.

Our bedroom is in ruins,
Your moans still fill up my ears.
We walked the pavements together
And wiped away all our tears.

All the paintings on our walls,
Of what we could have become.
We fell apart I knew we would
And happy thoughts we have some.

Leon Patrick Slater

Where Do I Find Love, Or Does Love Find Me?

Where do I find love, or does love find me?
I've begun to really wonder,
been down the garden and had a good look,
peered under stones and stood by the brook,
but no-one seems to be there for me?
why is it I find love isn't to be?
I've always worked hard and done my best,
so why am I left behind all the rest?
they all seem so happy and full of glee,
but why is it no-one seems to wait for me?
I smile and carry on day to day,
thinking that love must be on its way,
not to worry love finds you,
but maybe I'm supposed to help look too.
I brush my hair and take good care,
just in case someone stops to stare,
a real prince charming just like TV,
why is it I find love isn't to be?
But I sighed one day to the passing breeze,
where do I find love,
or does it find me?
it answered don't try just to please,
you'll find that love is quite a tease,
a sparkling eye and a happy heart,
that's enough to make the start.

Joanne Alison George

Visions Of The Soul

Like the first vision of sunlight,
To an awakening babies eyes,
A feeling unrivalled,
No words to describe,
An innocence so pure to behold,
One moment to steal for eternity,
Cherished to forever and beyond,
A warmth of joy to stir its soul,
Yet as that infant, so fresh to our world,
With eyes closed, and heart untouched,
When, with my sight darkened to light,
My thoughts not my own,
I hear the sound of your voice,
And the blindness of love is lifted,
A breath of soothing air,
Raising my dormant senses,
Shaking off the shackles of life,
An image of destiny,
Beauty so spellbinding,
A mere presence to invoke,
A radiance of the heart,
Or that momentary seizure of delight,
Drowning my veins,
Praying gently on my mind,
Visions of love,
A passion so divine,
As your words pass on the wind,
Like sunlight to that babies eye,
Scattered on the breeze,
And gathered by the angels,
Ready to tender my heart,
When the scene fades to black,
As darkness enwraps my dreams,
A lonely moment, that forgotten instant,

Then,
I feel a hand,
A hand reach inside my soul,
As they leave behind a gathered word,
And a distant reminder to me,
Why I love you so.

Peter Morris-Webb

Growing Old

There are many good things about growing old,
And I'm going to tell you a few.
First of all, you're allowed to forget
All the tasks you don't want to do.

You need only hear what you choose to hear,
Just look blank and tilt your head.
If they shout, then shed a tear,
They'll be sorry for harsh words said.

You only need see what you want to see,
Ignore all the grot and the grime.
Let others make life obstacle free,
All in the fullness of time.

They'll smile at you benignly,
Give you an encouraging nod,
What you must never let them know
Is you're a crafty old sod.

Christine Smith

24/7

In less than 24 hours
From elation to deflation
From euphoria and applause
On the streets of London
To sudden, forceful pause
Across the transportation network
From gasps of delight
To gasps of horror
From cheerful noise
To serene silence
Lives cruelly snatched away
Hearts leapt on Wednesday,
Sank on Thursday
Hope now sapping from the heart of London
And the heart of man
But my hope is in sovereign hands
As the nations rage,
My heart remains steadfast in One alone
8 men in a room can never save the world
Nor the words, deeds or music of man
But at the King's Cross
I still have reason to believe.

Anne M Carter

Frustration

Something inside me snapped today
so this poem my thoughts convey.

Sometimes I'm placid, even resigned,
but today I'm angry, tormented of mind.

Each day my alarm is set for eight
but **he** always gets up quite late.

He comes dressed smartly all in blue
while I, dishevelled, cook the 'stew'.

I wash the dishes, clean the hobs
and various other household jobs.

The meals are eaten - no praise or reaction -
Just taken for granted - no satisfaction.

There's washing and ironing every day,
Saturday, Sunday come what may.

Household chores are down to me -
He thinks it's not his job you see.

He thinks housework should be done by staff.
Four mornings, one lady - that's a laugh!

Does the food just appear on the shelves,
Supposedly put there by Elves?

He will wipe the dishes - don't get me wrong -
But-does he expect a medal or a gong!

There's hours and hours of office work,
I seldom relax and never shirk.

Yes-he dresses smartly, gets up late
Then disappears with his soul mate.

Do I sound bitter - Yes I do -
It's time to quit, find pastures new.

I yearn for a better life of bliss.
Life is too precious to waste like this.

Beryl Stone

Cat Burglar

There are many happy kittens
Who live here in our block
And all can come and visit me
'Coz my cat flap's got no lock
They're in and out both night and day
No privacy for me.
I wish they'd find another home
From which to nick their tea.
The food I leave for later on
Is never there for long
And when I feel the need to eat
I find that it's all gone.
I don't know who the villain is
But have some good ideas
She's ginger and she lives next door
And has done so for years.
So 'Tiffy' if I catch you miss
I'll stand for it no more
'Coz very soon you'll surely find
There's a lock upon my door.
Electro-magnet is the key
So I can live in peace
And from then on I hope to find
The nicking then will cease.
No matter how you wail and scratch,
Miaow or scream or shout
The door will never open
'Til it's me that's coming out.
Yes one fine day I promise you
You'll get the biggest shock
For when you come a thieving
You will find I've got me lock!

Ruth Laughton

The Dance

The dark descends,
Weary travellers
Waiting patiently in a queue
Observe the movements.
No more on board:
The bus is full.
The dance begins:
The bus pulls back;
Another round the corner
Reverses towards it.
Expert timing, daring driving
Smooth control, as one front swings round.
Pulling forward
Missing by inches
The next bus under
The traveller's frown.

Catherine A Gabbott

Believe

Love find the shards
that cut and shred my trust.
Encompass and hold
the jagged pieces that bleed.
Wince as the wound
deepens and progresses
but,
believe that you can stop it.

Hold me tight against the heat
generated between souls.
Hold me until we melt together
closing the rift
that has always been
within my troubled heart
and,
believe that you can heal me.

Nikki Anne Schmutz

She Is Lost

Granny was so small in her bed,
White sheets misted the air about her,
She lay surrounded by lino sore from over mopping.

There was a line of pink pain where a mouth should be,
How I longed for the "how big you are now".

It never came, though I strained my ears.
Fat unsalted tears fell and my body,
Seemed to melt to nothing.
About me the world closed in.

Everything was wrong- too clean.
My hand was bigger than hers and yet,
In my head she towered in love over my five year old frame.
The squishy warm comfort was gone.

Who had stolen Granny?
Why had they left a little old lady in her place,
When she was a dead giant in my mind.

Anna Isaac

Birthday

Today it's your birthday!
'Happy birthday, daddy.'
You can open this one
And I'll open all the rest.

A card is pulled from envelope
Scripted in flourishing aged hand,
Five pounds is wrapped and falls
From a card marked 'with deepest sympathy.'
'Here's thirty pounds toward your pension
And should be dry by the time it reaches you.'
Love your sister and family.
'Happy birthday, nephew!'
It's your yearly treat
Burn rubber as you ride in the red
Embossed sports car, just one more time.
Next year you play golf.

I feel no older; still have to go to work;
My candles are tasks to be snuffed out
One by one.
If today is my special day,
What shall I do tomorrow?

Curtis Tappenden

Waiting

The dust dressed the Earth, sown on by the wind,
As my heart is caressed, by the thoughts of the sinned.

The dirt homed the flowers, potted by time,
As my life passed in hours, to the sound of the chime.

The soil weaved a rug, shaped by the sea,
As my soul shuddered, at the thought of me.

The Clay formed the man, fashioned by our deity,
So I shall live, and wait, with anxiety.

Henry Warwick Parkin

He Sleeps

He had the hands of a child
I held him in my arms
He seemed as if asleep
He seemed as if just still
Taking without warning
Leaving me to weep
I held him in my arms
As if he were asleep.

Everything was his to have
I cradled him so tightly
He seemed as if asleep
He seemed as if just still
Taken without warning
I am left to weep
He lay within my arms
As if he were asleep.

We had so little time for us
I held him, held him close
He seemed as if asleep
He seemed as if at rest
Taken without warning
I'm sure he hears me weep
He is in my heart
As if he were asleep.

Tom Pheby

Don't Go Into The Barn

I said I'm doing it for the man I love
I'm doing it for the man I don't trust
And nobodies' words will convince me
Nobody can reassure me

Yes, I wish I were normal
Oh how I wish I were like you
I don't know why I'm like this
But I'm not insane
There are noticeable differences
Don't let go of my hand
And don't utter a word to her
For it will all be in vain

In a dream I saw She was dead
Dangling high from the ceiling of a barn
And the top end of my cane
Glazed her bare, paling skin

Yes, I wish I were normal
Oh how I wish I were like you
She was completely innocent
She was just passing through
Her eyes merely met yours
And nothing more came about
But her snapped neck makes me smile
Never again shall she be near you

Joe Gardner

Gilgamesh

Gog and magog, garlanded,
festooned, brought close
by penny'd thoughts, not
charity; marooned.

dread feelings, reined in
fresh, from summer's din,
Gilgamesh suffers bull's
great sin

to all the while be bold
but counted not, known but
profit not therein

past heroes wrenched by page
from truth, sooth the troubled,
modern death

soon spared torment's record,
past, distant wanderers into
myth so pass.

Peter Lewis Holmes

Do We But Dimly Perceive?

My form but dimly perceived by her dark pearls,
Born of the Indian Ocean's black abyss,
As her sweet-scented tsunami unfurls
About dusky aromatic shores of bliss.
Strange are the ways the minds-eye responds
To mundane stimuli – sights and sounds
That within each ear, like waves resound
And across iris flicker…ripples on ponds.
Her primordial tempests, untamed, on fire
Are far too oft to give unwonted rise
To my own long-lived and bitter ire,
And yet that elemental force soon dies
To give way to a strange malaise that drapes
As her sullen moods hang upon my shoulders,
But then lovers have long since worn such capes
And have done so in spite of all selfish desires.

Stephen Michael McGowan

The Heart

'tis but a cruel mistress
one day laughing
yet the next crying
should be one not both
could rest either way
but like to strain us it does.

likes to play folks to and throw
no thought for the mind it has
off one way then straight back
up and down - side to side
it has no cares.

a lover for us does the heart find
for the mind it doesn't mind
either rough either calm
no doubt we all like to drown.

Amy Culpepper

Eyes Of Suicide

Curtains not drawn,
Windows not closed.
Decided not to love,
The one who proposed.

Through the eyes of suicide,
Through the eyes of death.
Again I died,
As I took one last breath.

Hiding my tears,
From this sudden upset.
Hiding my fears,
From life's common threat.

I was pushed into this death wish,
And given no luck.
Unable to cheat, fail or pass,
In this life I'm stuck.

Elizabeth Price

Despair

Stripped of your soul. Your guardian angel left
to follow. Left you here bereft
and hollow. An empty shell on a busy beach.
That no one raises to their ear. No speech
could fill the void, avert you from your path.
Self-destruction looms. You fear no wrath
from a deaf god. Dead to your despair.
Oblivious to your screaming prayer.
The courage that you crave. At hand.
This selfish act, so long unplanned.
Now fills your mind. Crystal clear.
This final action, though severe.
That severs you from pain extreme.
May take you to the place you dream.
And standing now by the abyss.
Tempting. Alluring. Better than all this.
You jump. Exalting to be free.
Revelling. Briefly. Then enter your insanity.

Joseph Parks

Tiger Stripes

Tiger stripes upon my arm,
I never meant to cause this harm.
It slices like a butter knife,
Into which I throw my life.
Shredded like a child's graze,
When will I ever end this craze?
Tears roll down my sunken face,
How I wish I could flee this place.
My love of pain irks my soul,
How will I ever make me whole?
And then the cover up begins,
With trying patience wearing thins.
Wipe up, clean out and start again,
Nothing changes; it's all the same.

Lucy Ann Sparrow

Generation Gap

It doesn't matter you don't listen, or interrupt me while I'm talking,
It doesn't matter you don't look, or watch where you are walking,
It doesn't matter, you prattle on, until my mind goes numb,
It doesn't matter who just died, I didn't know your chum,

It doesn't matter who you've seen,
It doesn't matter where you've been,
It doesn't matter where you went,
It doesn't matter one percent.

It doesn't matter I suppose, what you've cooked or eaten,
It doesn't matter I suppose, who your team has beaten,
It doesn't matter I suppose, who you called, or who you saw,
It doesn't matter I suppose who knocked upon your door.

It doesn't matter who you've seen,
It doesn't matter where you've been,
It doesn't matter where you went,
It doesn't matter one percent.

It doesn't matter to the world, where you've been today,
It doesn't matter to the world, what you think or say,
It doesn't matter to the world, please listen, I implore,
It doesn't matter to the world; we've heard it all before.

It doesn't matter who you've seen,
It doesn't matter where you've been,
It doesn't matter where you went,
It doesn't matter one percent.

It doesn't matter your half cousins, daughter's son's just wed,
It doesn't matter your next-door neighbour's second wife has fled,
It doesn't matter you're repeating, what I've already heard,
It doesn't matter that you're mumbling, I didn't hear a word.

It doesn't matter who you've seen,
It doesn't matter where you've been,
It doesn't matter where you went,
It doesn't matter one percent.

What matters? You are always there,
What matters? You will always care,
What matters? Is what I've become,
What matters? Is that you're my mum!

Philip J Legood

Fit To Drop

I used to sit at home and knit,
But now I'm obsessed with keeping fit.
I tell myself 'I gotta keep slim',
As once again I head for the gym.

If I'm honest I'd rather go swimming,
It's better than dieting if you're slimming.
I plough up and down against the clock
In the hope one day I'll squeeze into that frock.

I pedal the bike with power and vigour,
It goes nowhere but it's good for my figure.
It's just so boring my mind goes numb,
But I think of what it's doing for my bum.

Have you ever wondered how a hamster feels
When it's running round in one of those wheels?
If you really want to know,
The treadmill is the place to go.

The leg press though is quite a winner,
I don't mind that if it makes my thighs thinner,
But the abdo crunch is a living hell
And I have to work out on that as well!

John says he loves me the way I am,
So when I'm digging into the jam,
I always try to remember that
He says I'm just cuddly and not really fat.

Joan L Defraine

The Outsider

Winging from place to place the welcome unfolds
The acknowledging nods from strangers
To me the stories are not told.

I could live my life in Ireland
I could while away the days
I could be a permanent outsider
But me this would not phase.

The depth of colour of the lakes
The mountains and the sky
I could be a stranger evermore
But the earth would welcome me when I die.

Lindsay Michael Hayman

The Last Big Sigh

I'm lying here,
I need to sigh,
To give my loved,
My last goodbye.

I am aware,
Of those around.
Both here from heaven
And earthly ground.

I need to look,
To see their faces.
Before I pass by,
And they give their graces.

I feel their love,
So deep within.
As they stroke my hair,
And my facial skin.

I have to go now,
To the place up high.
With loved ones greeting,
To help me by.

So here I go,
My last big sigh.
God Bless you all,
This is my Goodbye.

David Boyce

Addiction

You are like
A drug to me
A dangerous one
Only I can see.

I'm totally addicted
I need you every day
And if I do not have you
My mind begins to fray.

You and nicotine
Are the habits that I hate
I need to give you up
And find my true soul mate.

To give you up
Is near to hell
You make it so hard
-You're addicted as well

So let's go into re-hab
And try to change our minds
If I get out of yours
Will you get out of mine?

Ellen Jones

Letters In Faded Ink

Do you have love for the prey eerie palace,
where the Birds of Paradise flock around the nomadic pasture,
in the chamber massive and continuous.

Do you tourist the rooms and doorways,
obscure places and nod with satisfaction.

If not go deeper.

See moustaches and grins as you are swept up in a dance,
surrounded by a crowd of naked young girls.

Festival climax or ancient religion?

And you convert, increasing your complications,
lessened by the circle of dancers and dragon-like embers,
adding to the joyous chaos.

And with fondness to wine, ancestors and graveyards,
the goat ritual tribes a population to furniture at your celebration
hooves.

And you are infidel and cousin, neighbour and outlaw,
beckoned and offered baskets of berries,
nuts and dried fruit in the harvest of the glowing spirit.

And as a slave, block-by-block you entertain the gods,
playing a harsh journey,
building up structure and evidence of your creative capture.

And it is all sunlight and turquoise,
corn and stone as galaxies import plumage to help you fly further,
into dark fields of ingenious darker destinies.

Lee Richard Kirsten

The Mist Of Peace

I wander alone across English yonder
in search of..., 'is it peace?' I wonder.
Gazing bluntly over dewy skies
A drop of mist falls upon my eyes...
I blink to clear the moist of the mist
To find yet more cascade on my lids.
The rain sprays gently upon my face,
My lips, my hands in all its grace.
The place exudes me in all its glory
And here again, begins my story...

I wander alone across English yonder...

Alison Sutton

Love

Loves not just a feeling but an action too
You've got to show love for them to show you
It's not about poems and little sweet rhymes
It's about getting through all the bad times
You have to get along and talk about things
Then forever trust and loyalty it will bring
Cupid doesn't send an arrow, which makes love
So don't wait around for an arrow from above
Marriage vows mean lots too
But not so much to kids like me and you
We think about kissing on our first date
Not about serving them dinner on a plate
We don't think about jobs or Uni
More like boyfriends round for tea
We all say I want to be rich and cool
But I would rather be poor than a fool
Money can get you out of trouble and strife
But it cannot buy one ingredient in life
An emotion felt by every human being
It is an action that can be clearly seen
Not anger, jealousy, or green envy
Which is something most don't want to see
If you do not tell someone you love them so
Then they will never be the one to know
It does not matter if rich or poor
But if they'll love you forever more
So show our love and thoughts
Because love can never be brought.

Jemma Walker

34

Shadow

It follows you everywhere,
Yet not intended to scare,
Shares your shape, your size,
Only seen by your eyes,
It could be said,
It is a reflection of your soul,
A mirror image of your dreams,
And everything that makes you whole,
When you can't see it,
It doesn't mean it's not there,
Merely hiding,
In a million pieces in the air,
The closest to yourself you can get,
Is by understanding,
Your true silhouette.

Joseph David Perry

Oh Spring

Oh spring that you have come back once again
To greetings of cold hands and frosted speech,
Replacing touch of winter, your old friend,
Bid him goodbye with tulip handkerchiefs.
The crunch of bitter snow beneath your feet,
A sound that is forgotten as you paint
Soft scented shades of crimson, cream and peach,
With blended pastels knowing no restraint.
No mortal's hopeful heart shall ever taint
This canvas blessed by Venus' budding gems,
Entwined with songs of Muses and of Saints
That harmonize white bells on slender stems.
Soft breezes spread the calmness of your heart
And guide us to the peace found in your art.

Katherine Birchall

Trafalgar

Pools of blood they do surround,
helpless Sailors on the ground.
Lots of screaming,
what's the point we're not succeeding.
Listen to the deadly silence
for a minute ago there was nothing but violence.

Many ships went sailing past,
as the Sniper on the mast
shot Lord Nelson who was terrified
very sadly Lord Nelson died.
The terrible events that occurred
really aren't that absurd
for a war.

Bethany McIntosh

The Lighthouse

Hello, who are you?
You came to me over the sea
A wind in the storm
A presence so warm
You flew to me over the sea.

Oh, I stood alone
And too blind, on my own,
To see things that I wanted in life
Then a far away voice
So remote in the night
Was the one voice that helped me decide.

Oh, here I am standing
And so far away
But I access your subconscious mind
For like everyone else
I need sweet dreams at night
And I seek all the hope
I can find.

And you are my lighthouse
A voice in the dark
But shining your words loud and clear
A voice from afar
As remote as the stars
But your message abides with me here.

Oh, I stood all alone
And too blind, on my own,
To see roads I should travel one day
But the dark shadows cleared
And I walk without fear
Now the lighthouse has shown me the way.

Terry Pratley

In Lament Of Sundays

The days of my childhood
Where have they fled?
Sunday School Sundays
So quickly sped.
Quietly kneeling
Hands folded together
Dreaming of running
Through fields full of heather.
Days filled with sunshine
Seeming forever
Gone with those Sundays
Returning never
Friends of my childhood
Where are they now?
Out of town shopping
Where else - silly cow!

Dolly Chambers

Games Special

We gather in the lounge
For our brains to expound.
First a natter to unwind
Better to start with a clear mind
Game to centre for all to see
Will the starter be A, B or C
Eyes down, now to concentrate
Hope not to hear teeth start to grate.
'Cos one gets up very tight
Scanning around with all their might.
Damn, I had designs in that there
But, someone beat me by a hair.
Could've been a score of twenty
Still there are places aplenty.
Well it is only a game to enjoy
Even though I missed my last chance with 'Ploy'
Luck is really all one needs
When others, your brain wish to impede
Ooh! Another good chance gone 'Queen!'
'Cor hold it! Don't dare to scream.
Where can I put this 'B' thing
No time ever to babble
Have you guessed? Yes, it is Scrabble.

Edith Blagrove

Some Dorset Delights

Gently the wind blows on the fields.
Upon the long summer day.
Surprising, corn is ripe.
Beside the pub 'The Maid of May'
Is full of hanging red roses so bright!
Over the grass hill
Is to feel the breeze is so real.
As the clouds just roll by,
Full all magic greenery and sounds;
To catch the eyes of traveller's with happy children.
To see the beauty always buys a contentment-
How it lies.

Sammy "Michael" Davis

The Sea

The sea, the sea, the wonderful sea
With huge waves crashing onto the shore
Leaving stones behind with each retreat
But slowly advancing more and more

The off shore winds whip up these waves
Making white horses that dance and play
Pounding rocks again and again
Filling the air with a salty spray

No wall can contain this monstrous force
That's been trying forever with all its might
To overcome all that gets in its way
And take back the land as if by right

Rowena Haley

The Cottage

An out-cast cottage lonely stands
with lifeless life around it.
The chickens peck and lay their eggs
under windows that are never lit
by "Happy Lights" to say "Were Home".
All the tramps from miles around
pass many a night in shelter.
Convincing themselves that the dust is theirs
that holds a few years of history.
The rickety table and three-legged chairs
are signs of forgotten ancestry.
With pity, the sun, momentarily kind
Transforms the black stone to grey.
The windows will struggle to shine through the grime,
Then it fades with the light.
Obscurity,
Nothing.
A nothing to rot slowly to time.

Jennifer Miller

Grandchildren

When I was told I was going to be a Grandmother.
I was all of a to do
Not only have I got one
But now I have got two.

They are there to make you laugh
They are there to make you cry
I love to be with them all the time
And I don't know really why.

They seem to be a part of me
And they give me lots of joy
I love them to bits
My little girl and boy.

Grandmothers never forgets birthdays
They have a bedtime story to share
I would be lost without my grandchildren
And that I could not bear.

I love to take them out
And treat them all the time
I do love to spoil them
Because feel they are mine.

When they start to grow up
Have children of their own
I hope they will remember me
And all the love I have shown.

Barbara Jackson

Lessons Of Earth

We are all here thus to learn,
Today mine, tomorrow your turn,
Hope you will be around holding my hand,
Helping me in all, helping me to stand,
Lessons of earth at times very hard,
Not one of us from them ever barred,
Many the shoulder on which to cry,
Many the cuddle before we of earth die,
I may be here today, you on the morrow,
Picking up that of life's full sorrow,
If learning to give and thus to take,
A better place of this earth we to make,
We have love within our power,
Within each minute of every living hour,
We are what we are this said day,
What of the morrow can we say,
All needing each other to help us through,
In the many things having for to do,
I may need you, you may need me,
With love and thoughtfulness there to be,
So with our joining we will get through,
This walk of life's ways having to do,
All in this together, that's for sure,
Each of us knocking upon each other's door,
If knocking upon my door I will let you in,
For you and I throughout life will have many a sting,
We will forever always to be there,
Our laughter and worries in part to share.

June Annie Davis

You Stole My Heart

You stole my heart and made it yours
then let me down just like before
and when you said it could no longer be
I felt my soul die inside of me.

Dawn Morris

Torment

A tune rings out; it's from 'William Tell'
From two seats back rings a strident bell
The 'James Bond Theme' adds to the strain
Impossible to relax if you travel by train
On and on, peoples' voices drone
Each person using a mobile phone
No volume control, they all seem to shout
Thus solving nothing, they cancel each other out
Intimate details of their love lives are shared
To all and sundry, no one is spared
Latest news of assorted relations
Where they have been on summer vacations
Mind numbing subjects, so mundane
Can't avoid hearing them here on the train
Text message jingles, from earphones loud bands
Now I have started wringing my hands
All this noise could drive you insane
I'm thinking of pulling the emergency chain
Why oh why is there no rest for me
From all this endless cacophony?
This country we're told has a silent majority
Well, on this journey they're in a minority
Now there's a quarrel, two men start to yell
Have I no kindred spirits on this train from hell?

Calvin White

An Enchanting Winters' Day

It was a magical time out there last night
When all around was covered in light
The sky had burst open and spilled out the snow
And everything was shining as a radiant glow.

Across the field all is glistening white
Nothing to mar such a beautiful sight
Only the prints of a dancing bird
Or a baby deer that had roamed from the herd.

In the distance the church bells ring
And children on bobsleighs laugh and sing
Snowmen are appearing in every garden space
And snowballs are thrown all over the place.

The river is still flowing under the ice so far and wide
Carrying tiny icebergs in the grip of its tide
The overhanging branches from trees so bare
Have icicles dancing like crystals in the air.

The surrounding hilltops glint and shine
As the sun filters through the waving pine
It shimmers on the lake far down below
Where swans swim together to and fro.

All is quiet now the wind has passed away
A silent tranquillity of winters' day
All this will disappear in the warmth of a thaw
And the scenic panorama will be no more.

Phillis Green

The Lonely Hours

The lonely hours of night when all are lost in sleep
Save you alone, awake and wracked with pain.
The minutes how they dawdle, the hours slowly creep
Till dawn comes and you start a day again.

They ask you 'Did you sleep well? Have you had a better night?'
A stab of pain says 'Liar', so you won't forget it's there,
As you once more dissemble, hinting everything's all right
You don't say that it's all that you can bear.

There's a bustle all around you as the nurses come and go
Whilst you remain immobile, prisoner in your bed.
Then they wash you - like the baby days you knew so long ago –
As your helplessness keeps throbbing in your head.

When at meal-times you're not hungry,
they chide you 'This won't do,
You've got to keep your strength up! Won't you really have a try
To eat another mouthful?' But you know you'll only spew
If now you force food down. You're so low that you could cry.

Soon the pain returns and grips you like an ever-flowing tide
Bringing wave on wave of misery and woe
Till you wish that you could shout your ache,
yet still some scraps of pride
Now constrain you from just letting it all go.

Next you greet your healthy visitors, who soon run out of talk
As they press gifts upon you until you want to choke
Or they ask you stupid questions, such as 'Have you tried to walk?'
Or tell again some weak and pointless joke.

They go, and then the ward is slowly settled down
Till the staff-nurse turns to switch off the main light
And once again you listen as your fellows' snore and moan
As you face the lonely hours of one more night.

Jim Lawes

Prisoner

The prison of his window keeps air tight
The fairies though immobile take their flight
The trees beyond so distant fill his sight

The jailor of his spirit gives no place
The unsparing greenery holds key space
The boundary prickly hedged grasps his face

The dungeon of his thinking sinks so black
The ugly reeking gremlins bring his sack
The yawning twisting passage snarls come back

The torturer of his footsteps archscrapes there
The yellow jelly backbone bends his fear
The total awful 'thingness' ends all drear

Steve Mann

A Treasured Memory

I remember childhood days,
Idyllic summer holidays,
At Nan and Granddad's country cottage,
In that glorious, Devon village;
Every morning, up at six,
Mushrooms waiting to be picked,
Back at seven, breakfast waiting,
Add them to our eggs and bacon.
After breakfast, off we'd go,
In the warmth of summers' glow,
Through fields and woods and leafy lanes,
Stop by the bridge where under, trains,
Would heave and clank their way uphill,
'Midst clouds of steam, with sulphurous smell,
Then to the beach, where golden sand,
I used for building castles grand,
That filled my little heart with pride,
Then came the turning of the tide,
Which washed my sandcastles away,
And with them too, my childhood days.

Tony Reese

The Morning

Before opening my eyes I know it is
Morning. Dawn came silently hours ago.
Arms reach back, toes point forward
Ballerina-style to the end of the bed
And I stretch out like an accordion
With one long revitalizing yawn.

Downstairs the kitchen choir begins.
Washing machine starts a low note,
As though it is blowing into a bottle
Filled only a third with water.
Next the curtains delicately rattle
On the rail as they are opened.
Teacups sing soprano.

These are the quiet minutes of the day
When I can chase fast-evaporating dreams
Or begin to assemble the jigsaw puzzle
Of the day ahead.

This is the time I thank the bed
For cradling me for hours,
Thank the warm hair on the pillow
For cushioning me,
The Night for leaving so quietly
And the Day for remembering me.

Michelle Beech

The Brightest Star

I am writing a letter to my Daddy,

now I am five years old.

He lives in a place called heaven,

so I've been told.

I don't know where heaven is, or even how far.

But Mummy says he is all around, wherever we are.

How will he get my letter? I asked.

If he is never in one place?

He will read it as you write, Mummy replied.

With sadness in her face.

Now, my letter won't be very long,

as I have not long learned to write.

So, will Daddy think that I'm not very bright.

Mummy smiled and squeezed my hand.

You are *his* brilliance my love. And always will be

the very brightest star - in his heaven up above.

Christopher Smith

My Best Friend

My friend is the light
I cry if she is out of sight
Even when it's late
She is still a good mate.

She is great
And she is my best mate
When I'm down
She takes me to town.

If I have fear,
She helps me do a cheer
She may be nice
But she scares away the mice.

She is kind
And has a good mind
She is my mate
And I think she's great.

Sheila Smith

Options

To know that you're happy you must once had been sad
To know what is good you must know what is bad
To know what is weak you must know what is strong
And knowing what's right means you know what is wrong.

To value good health you must sometimes feel pain
In the same way that sunshine feels best after rain
To appreciate money you must know what its for
And to understand that you must once have been poor.

The best things in life are the free ones we're told
Though that's really no comfort if you're hungry and cold
But on the days when you're feeling warm and well fed
You'll not take it for granted but be thankful instead.

Life can be complex and much rests on fate
You learn to take chances before its too late
There's such a thin line between hope and despair
And little to choose between fair and unfair.

But in the matter of options there is really no choice
Inside each of us there's a single lone voice
It belongs to your conscience and won't let you be
Until you obey it, for then you'll be free.

Tony Wright

My Love

You brought meaning to my world again,
when you walked into my life.
Your smile, your touch, they eased away,
my troubles and my strife.

My awakening thoughts were all of you,
you filled my heart with joy.
I'd wrap my arms around you,
like I would, my favourite. Fluffy toy.

We've had our ups and downs we know,
but I've loved you from the start.
You were my one shining moment,
the one that took my heart.

If we hold on together, my love,
I know that we will cope.
And we will go from strength to strength,
for our future, there's some hope.

You do belong to me, you know,
in your heart you know it's true.
And me my love, what can I say,
my heart belongs to you…

Brenda Haines

Frozen In Time

Frozen tears upon my face
Like the cruel winter breeze
When summer comes around
My tears don't melt like the snow.

The hurt upon my face I can hide
But the pain will always be the same
Frozen in time I try to move on
I wish once more you were here.

Even for a little while more
So much has went on
And the time has gone by
Never to share it with you ever again.

Susan Brown

Mother Nature

I woke this morning feeling very sad
My spirits oh so low
But then I drew back the curtains
To gaze on the scene below
Trees were dressed in their finest greens
The sound of birds filled the air
The sun was shining from a clear blue sky
The world seemed at peace, without a care
We may often curse Mother Nature
When it's cold and the skies are grey
But we sing her praises on days like this
When all of her beauty is on display
She has the power to frighten us
As gales and storms often do
But the pleasure derived from her beauty
Is our reward for seeing it through
She has often been taken for granted
As man ravaged her beautiful scenes
Let us hope common sense will prevail very soon
And generations to come can enjoy lands of green.

Julia Boyle

Will Anything Be Enough?

This sickening warmth that is my stench,
floods the sight of my eyes so I am blind.
A tired mind harrows the rising damp of emotion,
aching in it's self to find its ocean.
No need to quiet unspoken thoughts temper,
expression is enough of a brutal trait.
A condescending quantitate of word vilely dear,
remains all the ears will hear.
Rejection of a slight fails to insight,
as fervent disappointment occupies all mind space.
A spoiled face the mirror will not always reflect,
haunts the heart of a reject.

Sophie Petrie

You Don't Care

Please believe me
When I say that you're pathetic
Please believe me when I say this.

You need to solve your problems
And get a life
To solve your soul and piece of mind.

You're not moving on as life goes by
Please say you'll try to care
Try to care today.

You walk alone through the gloomy night now
With not a thought of worry
You drink and drive as though it's not a problem
Please say you care, please say you care.

Tears flood the eyes of people around you
Scared for your life
Because of the way you are.

Please believe me
When I say you've got a problem
Please believe me.

Say you'll try to change and live life differently
Please say you'll try to care
Try to care today.

You walk alone through the gloomy nights now
With not a thought of worry
You drink and drive as though it's not a problem
Please say you care, please say you care.

Maria Jones

Fantasia

Ebony and ivory, lined up one by one,
Dusty tops in silent stillness sit.

A note is plucked, the dust disturbed,
The peace is shattered, note by note,
As fingers glide across the keys.

It starts out low, a bass note stroked
With gentle fingers, then it grows:
The right-hand joins, a slow crescendo
Climbing high, accelerando,
Scales and trills and chords to nourish
Frantic fingers reaching climax
One last pure accent then there's silence.

Trembling hands release the cover,
Stool pushed back, manuscript recovered.

Ebony and ivory, lined up one by one,
Left to long for hands so nimble,
Languish on their own.

Jennifer Elisabeth Mace

Angel

I look at her just laying there
I can't tell anyone what I fear.
I want to walk, walk away
I want so desperately to stay
Can I do this again, again,
Don't touch me, don't look at me
Leave me cocooned inside, while
I pray for her, breathe for her
She is untouchable, so unreachable
Never has anything been so loveable.
Four centimetres of glass one mile
for my heart.
I can't breathe, fear binds me.
I watch her little chest pulsate
First slow, then fast, then slow.
Eyes flicker behind closed lids
She wants to survive, I sense it.
She has fought longer than the rest.
Three days old, her battle strengthens her.
She has a chance they say!
I want to retch, to vomit to cry.
Many little souls came and went.
She lingers longer, grows stronger.
My body is damaged now barren.
She is my sole survivor.

Mel Moore

To My Rival

Oh God Her hair is all aflame
A Hindu goddess, she proclaims
Her five feet and Her smile
Seven inches wide
She is happy as can be
She is filled with ecstasy
She is 34 and sees
Nothing wrong with me
Turns Her face north-westerly
And takes his hand from Her knee
Now Her Best Friend drinks with me
And his hand is on my knee
So when everything that is She
Becomes everything that is me
My mind will be my mind again
When I cut all ties
And shrink in size
And take my clothes off in the rain.

Eleanor Dawn Howlett

Ballymore Holly's Gem
(for Frankie)

If I were there now, you'd certainly hear me neigh,
If I were there now, here's just what I'd say:
The first time I met you I was nervous; not real fear,
but you soon made me happy with your love so clear.

We both worked together, day by day training longer,
and as each week went by our teamwork grew stronger.
We both played together, we did well, had a good run;
we both had great fun, in the wind, rain and sun.

At first we were tentative, not too sure of our timing,
but as each month passed by all could see we were winning.
When I arrived at The Grubbins I'd already come far,
But, truly, thank you Frankie, You made me a STAR.

All my life I was moved, made to wander and roam,
but then, when I found you, I just knew I'd found home.
If I were there now, I'd have so much to say.
If I were there now, we'd probably just play.

If I were there now, you'd be fussing over my rug.
If I were there now, I know that we'd hug.
It's nice here, I'm happy and not far away.
It's nice here, they like me, I just heard them say:

'Rubies, Emeralds and Diamonds they call precious gems,
but surely they're no match for Ballymore Holly's Gem!'
I'll always be with you, in your heart, by your side,
and Frankie, <u>I promise</u>, I'll be there when you ride.

If only I could talk to you, I'd say it's OK,
But as I can't talk, I'll be content just to neigh.
If I could have said goodbye, I'd have told you don't cry;
Be happy for me Frankie, and hold your head high.

If I were there now, that's what I'd say.
If I were there now, you'd surely hear me neigh!
Well guess what? I am home, And I've something to say:
'Shh, close your eyes now, don't cry, See:
You CAN hear me neigh?'

Chris Judge

The One

A feeling of true happiness a whirlwind of emotions
that has twists and turns like a roller coaster
being embraced within your loving arms
I feel safe and secure with you
I am complete like the final piece of a jigsaw puzzle
to me your are a sight of pure delight sun razes
that shine from your loving tender heart
that shines into me with you I feel
I'm able to achieve anything your love
elevates my mind, body, and soul
to a whole new dimension filled with kindness and joy,
every little thing about you I adore from the way you walk
to the way you talk even when you get in a strop
you still look beautiful and wonderful to me
your sense of style is enough to drive men wild,
eyes so innocence that they dare tell a lie,
lips that taste sweet but with a different flavour
every time when I hold your hand and hold you in my arms
I can feel our unborn child deep within you
to me you are nothing but a miracle
and I thank God for sending me an angel from up above.

Labi Hassan

Unlikely Eden

It's a fairytale all of it's own.
Dark tree tunnels with slender trunk walls
Hours and hours of play amongst grey jutting stones.
I hope they didn't mind the thundering of childhood feet
Six feet below in wooden beds so close to the earth.

Sunlight filters through leafy layers
The day the cadets came with their axes saddened me.
Gone were the winding tree hideouts
Places of play so deftly dismissed.
It's better when left to grow so wild and untamed.

Barefoot made it all the more fun
Feeling for a while like a person not from this time.
I lost count of how many brambles bit my feet.
A dainty little dance done to try and avoid them.
In the bath soles so black from dirt.

My own sorrowful secret garden
But somehow the graves don't dampen my spirits.
Little brick house, a cornerstone in a key place.
The rule to apologise when your feet strayed above
A sleeper's grassy quilt.

So, so beautiful. No neighbours.
Just birds, trees, flowers, stone
Elaborate rich family marble tributes
And forgotten flaked unloved patches.
Here, it doesn't matter who you were.

Because here is the place of nature
Here they lie all the same.

Amy Barnes

Hidden

I'm looking out the window,
the view is no surprise.
It's now what I see daily,
one hundred million eyes.

I stare at staring coldness,
their glare passes straight through.
Familiar as it may be,
I still can't tell who's who.

Now wading in the madness,
it's you I need to find.
But all these eyes still watching,
mask your hidden side.

Their view upon me alters,
as I crawl back to the dark.
They cannot see or reach me,
so I stay here in the past.

Olivia Atkinson

I'm Lost

I'm lost, and in my despair,
I turned down a map.
I haven't learned how to read you see,
So what good would a map be to me?
Because my teachers didn't like me.

I wore a 'hoody', I was not a goody, goody
Not bloody likely.
Never mind I don't care now,
It never goes my way.
So I might as well lose it.

Kathleen Bartholomew

The Rose

A rosebud in spring awakened
by fresh morning dew,
ready to bloom,
each petals edge curling back
slowly revealing a delicate beauty
like that of a lovers skin.
Soft to the touch and giving pleasure
to the senses, pure and simple.
Natures gift releasing a delicious scent,
subtle and fragrant, oh for that moment.
Dawn brings new-life, a truly inspirational sight.

Robert Martin Ricketts

Why Oh Why

Why oh why do I continue to wade
through the swamp of attachment
when a path has been revealed
Why do I not simply cut these bonds of sorrow
with the sweet reason passed on to me
Why do I continue to pursue short lived
sensual pleasures at the expense of eternal gains
Why do I turn away from the comfort
in truth and choose the road to pain

It is the material illusionist don't you see,
seeking to bury the soul I know myself to be
Tricking me into thinking that this body
and it's expectant senses is the true me

Having searched I have found the most valuable Jewell,
the golden key to unlock my higher destiny
Surely I cannot cast it aside,
surely whilst it sparkles before me I cannot continue to hide

An act of profound will I must summon to rise up
and take what's on offer to me,
I need to attain the answer to my pain.
I need to set myself free.

Michael John McCarron

Components

Harry had a computer
Who's mouse had broke.
How could he play his favourite game
In the morning when he woke?

His Gameboy needed charging
Before he could play Shrek.
The x-box wasn't chipped yet
and TV just ain't high tech.

The DVD player worked ok,
He just couldn't see
The latest copy version of
This weeks MP3.

The choice that Harry made
To entertain himself for the day;
Was to watch and learn from his Dad
on his Playstation as he play!

Dolly Parker

Chance To Live

Death is not fair
It has no sense of justice
Death that you do not choose

Life is not fair
It has no sense of justice
Life that you do not choose

Is our sense of urgency an illusion?
Are we congratulating ourselves for good luck
While shutting our minds to the unlucky?

To live well - what is that?
Connection, relationship, love
Plan, Act, Reflect

To die well is surely not
Disconnection, distance and hate.

Does loving life give death power
Or does a life well lived mean
Connection, relationship and love remain?

But no plan, no action, no thought
No worry, no tiredness, no pain.

Rachael Carrick

A Winters' Day

Each winters morn I wake to find that day is still the night,
And as I stretch the slumber from my limbs,
I see a glimmer, a distant light,
Through the window, far away, beyond the naked trees,
A newborn watery sunrise cautiously appears.

The cold wind whistles eerily, a gate swings back and forth,
The cat comes in for shelter from the shivers of the north,
And as the fire roars in the hearth, the snow begins to fall,
I hear the children playing as they get the winter call.

The snowmen greet me with stony smiles as I walk the frozen path.
The ducks are skating on the pond; one takes an icy bath,
The white sky meets the snow horizon to create a winter canvas,
Where nature paints a seasonal scene of people as they pass.

The cars and buses make their way slowly on the road,
And people fill the air with mists, as breath meets freezing cold,
The reddened cheeks of children, on their way to school,
Making snowballs excitedly and sliding on a frozen pool.

The day goes by as everyday in summer, spring or fall,
But when it's done at winter time I get the childhood call,
To frolic happily in the snow and play like times of old,
Getting soaked and never even noticing the cold.

A hot bath and a mug of tea leave me with a smile,
And as the dark returns for night I close my eyes awhile,
I dream of winters past that seemed to last for ages,
I dream about the book of life as seasons turn the pages.

Glenn John Walker

Dimensions Of Mind

I can't find the keys so I am
Locked in the cell, in
My own room's walls with
No window, not even
A pigeon hole to let some
Light in. Darkness
Crawls over everything
Slowly digesting me.
It is as if the Sun is
Wearing a veil, a mask.
I start to weep, but I know
It wouldn't help so I reach for the
Bottle of vodka and drink it
Till the very last drop.
It burns my blood.
I hear myself scream it
Seems music to my ears,
Yet someone's singing:

Think of love,
Dance in enchanted world,
Close your eyes,
Listen to the music of my voice.

He haunts me, sometimes,
It's so bad, I, even in my sleep.
Hear him, he whispers in my ears.
I awake and find myself lying in
The middle of the road

Dead.

Anna Kompaniets

The Miracle Man

Have you seen the miracle man,
The elusive miracle man;
For I need the touch of his magic hand
To chase away my troubled sense.

The Priest

Yes, I have seen the miracle man,
The elusive miracle man;
See, there, he hangs on that wooden cross,
He'll soak up all your sorrows.

The Rishi

Yes, I have seen the miracle man,
The elusive miracle man;
See, there, the one with the elephant head,
He'll protect you from harm and death.

The Billionaire's servant

Yes, I have seen the miracle man
The elusive miracle man;
See, there, he lives in that massive mansion,
He'll keep your woes at a distance.

The Scientist

Yes I have seen the miracle man,
The elusive miracle man;
See, there, he works in that lab,
He'll soothe your strained mental web.

The Philosopher

Yes, I have seen the miracle man,
The elusive miracle man;
See, here, he lives in your mind
He is your true miracle man.

Mahesh Patel

Hurt

It's time to give in, where do I begin.
My heart is aching my heads in a spin
Erase this feeling that holds me within.

To fight with your self as you look in the mirror
The warmth you once had grows dimmer and dimmer.
The words are so bad the claws so deep.
You cannot face the world you cannot sleep.

The path maybe long from where you are now
We struggle, move on and get through it some how.
It makes us much stronger and much more aware.
a lesson we must learn to help us prepare.
Just in case it should strike us again.
Then from its sting we will refrain.

Claire Ann Wall

Lost Soul

Do you love me?
The question of a lost soul,
Lost in time,
Lost in her mind,
Not knowing you,
Not knowing herself,
She asks the question, 'Do you love me?'
The answer is easy, 'Yes', a white lie,
You hardly know her,
How can you love here?
But, how can you say no?
To say no is to break her heart,
To bring tears,
To bring sadness,
At least while she remembers,
To say yes is to bring a smile,
To bring happiness to a tortured soul,
To bring a moment of contentment,
Until,
Her thoughts are lost in her mind,
All is forgotten…by her at least.

Lucy Beams

Where Is My Love?

Where is my love of yesterday?
The heartache will not go away
Memories that I hold dear
Fade a little with each year.

Was it perhaps all my fault?
If by some deed or a thought
I lost the love that I hold dear
And now I shed a silent tear
For my love of yesteryear.

Trissie Burgess

One Lost Soul

One lost soul she is now.
Me with the soul that has gone missing
The friend, my friend gone forever.
Will I see her again?
No never.
She is the missing cherry on my cherry cake.
The missing puzzle piece,
The missing part of me.
She follows me around but makes no sound,
the ghost that does not wish to be found.
My ability to laugh and smile
is now gone much further than a mile.
Her dull soft skin,
Her thin darkish lip.
The deformed nails of a friendly hand
Does now lie still and not stand.

Caroline Heywood

The Green Blanket Beneath My Feet

Is this my home?
What is a home anyway?
Somewhere to lay your head at night.
Or a pile of bricks which you so say own.

Well I have visited several places in my time
But never have I felt the way I feel now
Like the missing piece of a jigsaw has been found
Or a child has found its favourite toy.

Is this strange I ask myself?
No, I have the country in my blood
Or are the memories of my childhood still hanging in the present day?

Well I will find out in good time
Whether I am a natural roamer
No place to stay to long
For the unknown is my home today.

Clare Lynda Hayman

Aching

Aching alone with this manic pain
Laughter, hysterical laughter imprisoned inside.
Wails from that far off land, death calls
Again and again, repeats of reality,
You, staring, empty blank eyes, so distant.
So here I am, let me help?

As you whirl in uncertainty,
Nobody knows
Don't shut me out.

False lives under a shrouding lie
Old smiles fade, flicker and go out,
Resounding echoes shake the ruins.
Everything, everyone is a shaded blur.
Vicious needles of something unknown,
Easing off, away, escaping
Rosy cheeks turn pale and sallow.

Lucy Quarrier